INTERIOR 1

COLORING BOOK

Coloring Test Page

This coloring test page is a great way to practice your coloring skills and experiment with different techniques. Place a sheet of card or scrap paper behind to prevent bleeding.

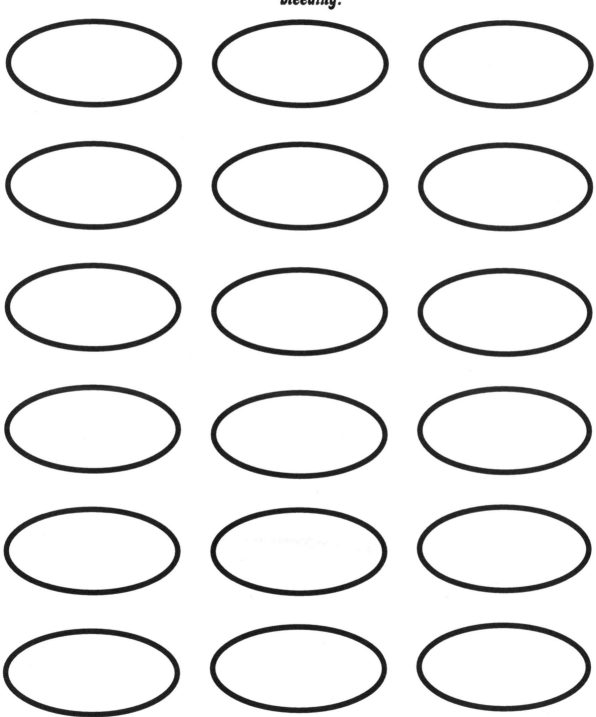

Shop our other books here!

Thank You!

Thank you for choosing our small business! We would greatly appreciate it if you could leave a review. Your feedback is important to us and helps us to improve. We value your support!